Congrats Grad!

To: _____

From: _____

D1404197

You'll learn a bunch of new stuff,
That's stuff you didn't know.
I hope you're not insulted;
You just look a little slow.
I bet you're excited,
Excited to grow.
Get up and get dressed,
Come on now, let's go!

Into the world we're off,
This is going to be cool.
We're going to learn shit they don't teach you in school,
Like how to do your taxes!
Yes, that's a big one;
It's highly important to life in the long run.
Before you learned Trig or writing in verse
Someone should've said "Hey, learn this shit first!"

Good old Uncle Sam
Always gets a cut.
Right from the top,
Without an, if, and or but.
How much does Sam want?
A whole fucking lot!
Just pay it up front; give it no second thought.

Why pay, you say,
All your hard-earned cash?
Because they'll lock your ass up,
And won't bat an eyelash.

Oh, yes! Off to prison is where you'll go;
Uncle Sam really wants you to cough up that dough.
He needs that money for different stuff;
Without it I'm pretty sure things would be rough.

It goes towards schools
and welfare too;
Some people are stuck
to their welfare like glue.
Now don't be judgmental!
No, judging is crude
It's tough to be poor
so let's not be rude.

Now back on the subject,
To the matter at hand:
Learning what to do to silence the tax man.
You've just got to pay him;
It's simple as that.
Use a tax prep company; their fees are flat.
You can also go online and do it yourself,
Or grab software from a local store shelf.
Find someone who does it—
For a living I mean.
But act like a vet. They sense when you're green.

You don't want to get stiffed,
At least I think not.
Some sneaks rob you blind
and won't even get caught.

You've got to be smart,
Intelligent even.
You guys are the future,
You're what we believe in.

Well you've paid Uncle Sam and now you're broke.
You have an internship? Yeah that shit's a joke
The time for that's passed! You're a graduate now!
You need to make money and you need to know how.
If there is no pay,
Those jerks have a glitch,
And last time I checked your parents weren't rich.
Someone's got to feed you, and pay your bills,
Unless you plan to work at night selling cheap thrills.

Most people get a job;
That's the easiest way.
But if you want to do that then you need a resume.

Have a seat, please, and re-type this shit.
All the nonsense and dumb stuff, you can omit.
Write about things you learned in school.
With detail; that's the golden rule.

Done nothing of note?
Add a little fudge.
If you've testified in court
simply say you helped a judge.
It's not really lying;
Wording is the key.
Like saying "No Contest"
for your guilty plea.
It's all the same but one sounds better;
Are you wearing a knit top?
Or just a damn sweater?
See my point? You need a way with words.
But don't go so far as to sound absurd.

Now the interview process;
This one's a kicker.
Put down the marijuana and lock away the liquor.
You need your whole head, your full concentration.
Getting this job means parental liberation.

Before you arrive, prep answers to questions,
Walk in, sit straight, do take my suggestions:
Listen, show interest, and don't slur your speech,
And don't talk too much, unless they've asked you to preach.

At the end, they'll smile and you smile too,
Show them the friendlier version of you.
Shake their hand firmly,
keep your head held high;
When they say "I'll be in touch,"
simply say that you'll reply.

You should always be sure

and you need to stand tall.

You're one hell of a person,

So don't act small.

Don't want to get a job?
Is that what I heard?
You can start your own business
like Mark Zuckerberg.
Anyone can do it, anyone at all,
But it won't be easy; most start with a crawl.

A simple idea inside of your head,
Until it's so strong it keeps you from bed.
Up thinking all night, about making it real,
And all of the fun, how good it'll feel!

If you keep up your faith,
Lock your eyes on the prize,
And travel the road, all the lows and the highs,
Success will find you at some point, I'm sure.
Don't believe me?
Just ask any entrepreneur!

Those are the two best ways to make money,
Unless you're extra pretty, talented, or really funny.
Then you'd have options,
Other things to explore.
**Who cares what key you use;
just open up the door!**

Oh, the shit you don't know,
Could fill a whole room!
A room that can hold a large army's platoon,
And that's why we're on this little learning spree.

The DMV, good friend, is a very sad place.
Where nothing's more rare than a smile on a face.
It's always packed, like an Irish bar,
And deals with most things concerning your car.
The lines are long, the employees are sour,
They get one lousy break and it's only an hour.
Barely enough time to eat or send a text,
And their whole day is spent yelling, "Who's next?"

Frustrating, of course, but it's what they must do.
They're there first for a check and second for you.
Keep this in mind when you're standing in line,
Pick up the right forms, fill them out, and sign.

When you get to the front,
Make sure all is in order,
Or the clerk will show symptoms of Bipolar Disorder.
They'll flip out on you, maybe huff and puff;
They really expect you to know this stuff.
They'll say "Step aside, and do it correctly,"
They'll give you directions, and they'll give them directly.

It's okay for you to feel a little ashamed;
It's your first go-around,
It's a part of the game.

Don't like the DMV?
Hate chopping through the thicket?
You won't go there much,
Unless you don't pay your tickets.
Your tags are once a year;
Renew your license every five,
But if you've got the ticket bug,
You'll need them to survive.

To prevent this, it's best
Not to get them at all
You don't need to send that text;
You can wait to make that call.
Speeding's your thing?
Better slow your ass down;
Going too fast might make a cop frown.

If you get pulled over,
Blue and red flashing lights.
Keep your hands where they can see them,
Especially at night.

Now I won't tell you much,
Or go into detail.
We want to avoid it,
So we won't discuss bail.
Just keep your nose clean,
And follow the road rules,
Or you'll end up cleaning trash outside of high schools.

So we've learned about money,
And about the DMV,
The rules of the road,
What about family?
Love, dating, marriage,
and all of those things;
Buying flowers and candy
and maybe wedding rings.

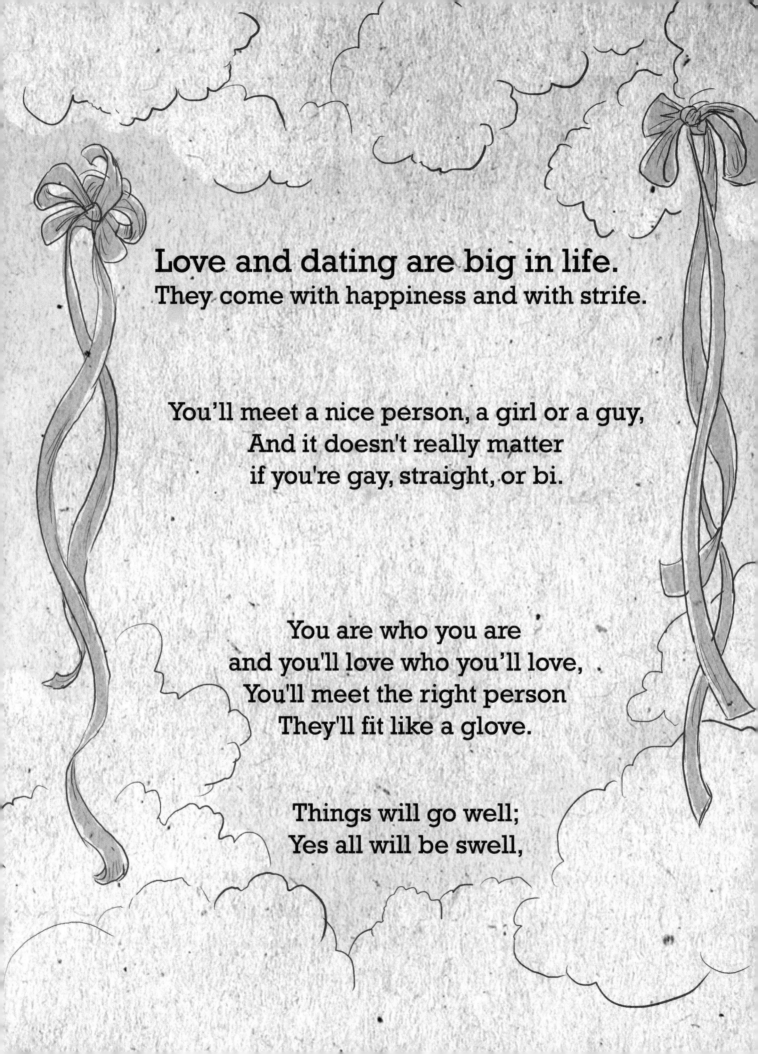

Love and dating are big in life.
They come with happiness and with strife.

You'll meet a nice person, a girl or a guy,
And it doesn't really matter
if you're gay, straight, or bi.

You are who you are
and you'll love who you'll love,
You'll meet the right person
They'll fit like a glove.

Things will go well;
Yes all will be swell,

In that case it's different, scary some say!
There are crazies lurking everywhere much to my dismay.
A crazy is a person, who doesn't know their cracked.
It's like their brain has gone away or maybe it's been hacked.
They do things like hit you or call you bad names.
Stop picking up your phone,
They'll say you're playing games.

They prefer for you to be,
Attached to their hip.
No clubbing for you!
And forget about that trip!

A lot of it is rooted in their own low self-esteem;
Trying to talk it out is like paddling upstream.

What to do with a crazy,
Once you've got one, you ask?
You leave them; be careful, it's no small task.

You don't want to be stalked, cut, shamed, or harassed,
Or have this relationship end up as your last.
You've got to be gentle with a crazy's feelings;
If you dump them too quickly they might hit the ceiling.

Let them down easy,
Slow and steady wins the race.
And if they start to yell,
walk away to save face.

Walk backwards at first, then turn to a trot;
Just in case your ex is more violent than you thought.

My mother always said keep your enemies in view—
Especially a nut, you never know what they'll do.

I held on to her words,
As you should hold these.
Remember what you've read here,

and life will be a **breeze!**

Okay, that was a lie,
but this is shit you need,
Unless you plan on being broke
or getting your car keyed.

There's still more to learn, and it'll be a blast,
As you sift and sort through all life's contrast.
Don't be frightened!
No, don't you fret,
Because you are not done learning yet.

Knowledge will find you
just when you need it,
If you remain open
and rise to receive it.

Remember this as you walk that stage,
And open your book to an awesome new page...

Life is indeed what you make it, my friend.
I'd suggest you make it great,
Right up until the end.

Autographs

Autographs

Autographs

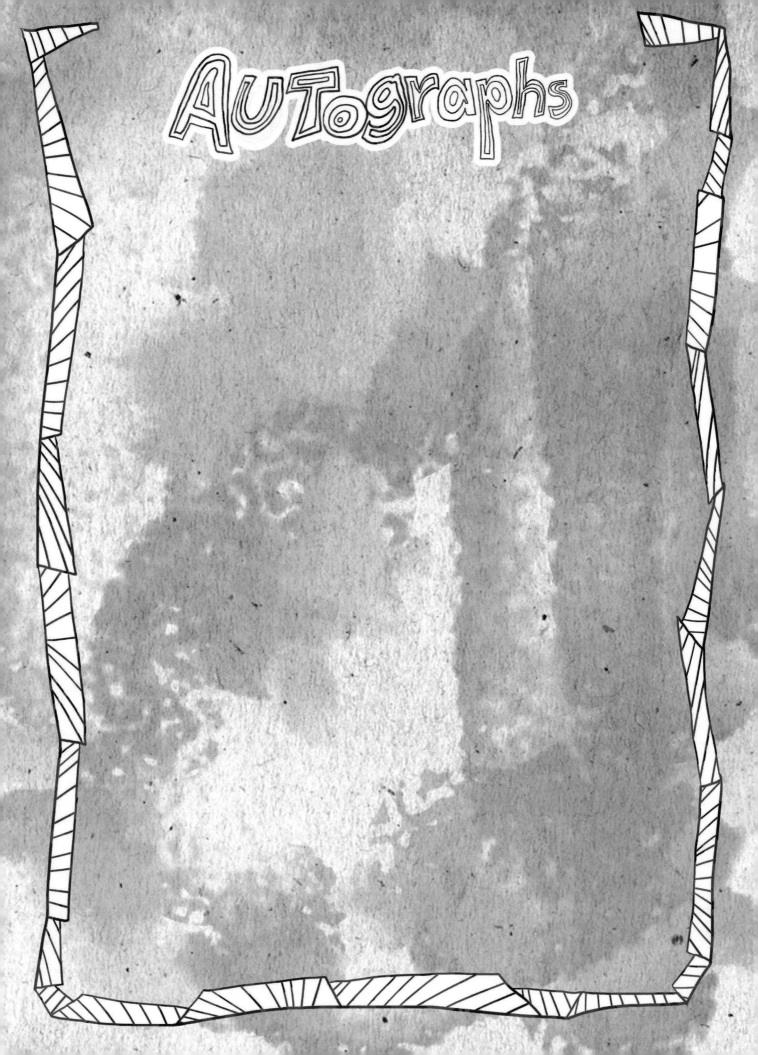

Autographs

Made in the USA
Lexington, KY
05 May 2017